Your Rhythm and My Blues

Tai Timmerman

BookLeaf Publishing

Presentation by *BookLeaf Publishing*

Web: www.bookleafpub.com

E-mail: info@bookleafpub.com

ISBN: 9789357440790

First edition 2023

DEDICATION

To my 17-year-old former self, who would have never thought about writing a poetry book. For my precious Writer's Guild family, the amazing Caribbean Student Association, my intelligent Robotics Club family, and my fabulous Alternative Spring Break Philadelphia partners at the illustrious Howard University. To the inspiring teachers and faculty at Bishop Kearney High School and Salve Regina Catholic Academy, the lovely Guyanese Girls Rock Foundation, my strong-willed Tishman Speyer DC Team from Project Destined, and my supportive friends and family. Lastly, to all of my godchildren.

ACKNOWLEDGEMENT

Writing a book is as hard as my major, yet it's more rewarding than I could ever imagine. None of this would have been possible without Mrs. Arlene and Mrs. Ronacher, two prominent women in my life. Mrs. Arlene cultivated my passion for writing and Mrs. Ronacher always pushes me to try new horizons no matter how scared I was.

I'm eternally grateful for my family: My mom, who never gave up on me, even when I wanted to give up. She taught me the importance of discipline and respect. One life lesson, I will never forget is to always knock on any doors with opportunities. The least they can say is "no". I had no idea where I would be if I did not take this lesson with me to college. My brothers, Tyler and Trent, you two have sustained me in ways that I did not know that I needed, especially with your two's sense of humor. Lastly, my grandma and grandpa. They always knew the right words to say whenever life does not go my way. P.S.: I miss the cooking tremendously.

To my awesome writing buddy, Jaylin Boykins, he read early drafts of my work and gave me encouragement to publish this book. He was as important to this book getting done as I was.

A very special thanks to Angel Bryant, the president of the Writer's Guild, at Howard University who encouraged me to take my poetry to the next level by sharing my passion for writing with the world.

I'm forever appreciative of my friends at Howard, specifically, Jaden Lopes Da Silva, Kamryn Hatcher, Soleil Warren, Abigail Lindo, Samaya Vaz, Mekhi Green, and Reaux Peters-Roussell. Along with my friends back home, Marykate Rosa, Ronnie Gonalez, Jaharie Waterman, Sofia Vanderpool, Sean Jennings, Elani Reyes, Brandon Cuevas, Saraí Cepeda, Aicha Barry, Richelle Holmes, and Kalind Gipson—I love you guys Ultimately, I am pleased with all of my friends and co-workers from the Van Dyke Community Center.

Finally, to the BookLeaf Publishing Company, I am blessed by your mission to discover new talent. Without this company, I would not have been able to publish my first book at 20 years old.

PREFACE

This idea hit me in the face recently to create a poetry book a year ago. Do not worry no one was hurt during the writing process.

Ok, maybe I was. That's only because of the start of my sophomore year. My tank was on E, yet my love for poetry filled me up.

The Fall Semester got me thinking about healthy ways to deal with my time, besides sleeping. Yes, sleep is important, but I wanted to do something challenging and fulfilling.

So, on October 15, 2022, I told myself that would write poetry every day at 9:30 pm before my bedtime. Now, whether or not all of you want to laugh at me for having a 10:00 pm bedtime, that is on you.

Life is too short to not write about the beautiful things of it. I say this to say, whatever all of you want to accomplish in life, just do it and tune out the noise. Inspiration comes in many forms and that is simply why I wanted to write a book with poetry–to connect with others.

Crack Epidemic

I've grown to love you. I love your zingy, bitter taste, floral smell, and the jolt of energy you give me. I knew I loved you from the start. Glancing over at your white coruscant crystals to the intense feelings of euphoria when I am around you.

Addicted to the sexual arousal of our skin touching each other. Always under the influence making love to me. Enter into my bloodstream. Inject me with your poison. I know you're atrocious for me, but it's too hard to let go of you.

Snort, smoke, and inject— repeat the cycle like a 6-carbon ring. Even though the high lasts 10-15 minutes, I feel as if I'm on cloud 9 for an eternity.

They say crack is a "rich man's" best friend until the CIA planted crack in Black communities. It never needed documents or passports to enter this country. Many have been murdered by crack and the government. Some are still reliving the physical and psychological trauma through their veins, a highway to generational curses, and a false sense of security.

Doped up with dopamine and a psychedelic prowl, my children may never get to see my vibrant personality, unless I am physically closer to heaven while having withdrawals. I want to stop, but crack is calling my name. I hope they understand when they get older that I was systematically oppressed and abused by the U.S. government.

Gang Related

There are too many blessed angels on caskets and not enough tears to cry a Nile River. They say “you only live once”, but you only die once as well. Either that or your body is put in a Rikers’ Island jail cell. No amount of bars that I write will remove the agony behind your sentences.

Multiple graves six feet underground with untold stories of their death. Silence, drugs, and violence are the biggest killers in America but she has the nerve to have her hand out begging for money like the Statue of Liberty.

Liberty to kill, rob, and steal by any means necessary and all of life’s traumatic tragedies stick up like the needle used to line your pockets up with grief and your pugnacity.

Instead of smoking the pain away, you rather smoke body swishers. Burning your soul with the intention to poison your Black brothers and Black sisters is a form of self-destruction.

The truth of the matter is when you rep your colors there is no turning back. I know you got stabbed a bunch of times so your back is looking as if you're a hedgehog. Defending yourself out of horror and anxiety, you scribe your loved one's name in the sky with the revolver that is on your hip. You have the liquor, but do not have the courage to step away from the hand that's feeding you the junk from a trauma bonding mechanism manual.

You step into the streets where there is no love and loyalty, and now the attempt to seek power and control is in a black duffle body bag. That same bag you put your opps in. That same man who was a son, father figure, and loving husband who didn't make it home tonight.

Guns and Roses

No one is safe in the city of guns and roses, which breaks our bones and turns our ashes into stones, but when will we realize the pain and anguish of families writing their sons–daughters–cousins—uncles—aunts—friends—grandparents' name in the sky and on a tombstone?

Enough is enough!

I do not like the idea of pity prayer for situations that involve politicians who are supposed to be protecting and serving the people, yet as we speak, we are being served a platter with lies, blood-stained shirts, white doves, and clouds, and R.I.P's and, S.I.P's, but a lot of us are sleeping in war, not peace.

Weak in the knees, whimpering and screaming for justice. It's just us feeling the bullets pierce through our bodies like the Fourth of July—fireworks of celebration for bounty hunting— their bodies bleed out red and are beaten until they are black and blue.

I wonder about a world with no guns and roses. The rose petals are on the streets of the deceased at the crime scene, as yellow caution tape desensitizes our emotions into a puddle of the Nile River.

There are not enough angels in this world—not enough tears to cry—not enough flower petals to place over the grave sites of many bodies—not enough grim reapers to reap the benefits of death,

As we are scared to death to enter our surroundings with our eyes closed. All we can see are bodies and body bags dropping left and right of the red light on a corner.

Late Nights

Sometimes during dating, nap dates are a thing where
I sleep on the number of things you could provide for
me.
Your emotional support
swept me off my feet into the cold winters of
Toronto,
yet warmed the icicles off my heart and the frostbites
off of my fingers of selfishness.

The candy taste of your lips entices me
to go on an adventure to Take Advantage Town,
although it was not my intention.

My mind is spinning around and around and around
like a carousel to fight all of the flights,
while my fears of our relationship drown.

Driving on the interstate watching the
magical horizons, listening to music,
laughing at my jokes—to stare into your
amber eyes of security, as you hold me…

To never let go of me.

Lessons From My Replacement

I—
I was colder than Coldstone towards you but enjoyed the taste of your creamery. I was the Satanic hot environment that turned your growth into wilted greenery. I was the one who did not want you to reach your destination of harvest out of jealousy, so I altered your travel itinerary.

I—
Would you believe me if I said I would take the blame, catch a bullet or a grenade, and protect you from the inferno of a burning plane?
Probably not.
And I take accountability for my actions, but I do not want to write my wrongs—get left because I never acted right—or put this into a song but—

My words stung your heart with acid. The way I walked to you was passive and my tongue could get aggressive, but it's only because I loved you, yet I never showed it.

I can dish out my momma's cooking on Saturday nights in my grand momma's kitchen; I can dish out my uncle's famous deviled eggs; I can even dish out my delusional expectations for us—drag you through the mud by your hair, but I can't… I can't get served at a table full of reciprocity--whether good or bad.

Even though you never told me your exit plan, your body language shows me there's someone taking my place. Now he's sleeping on the same side of the bed where I once slept. Where the sheets held our secrets—where our pillows could talk.

I guess—
I guess there's nothing I can do now, but be upset at these four walls of imprisonment and myself.

My God—
he even took you out on dinner dates and ate it off of you, clean like a porcelain dinner plate. Plates of gold from your head down to your toes bought you bouquets of roses, and expensive clothes. He danced with you in the rain and cupped your face. I've seen him speak life into you outside of my window. That was the first

time I've seen you smile since you were with me.

I can never get you back because I treated you like a peasant. I treated you like the trash of the streets of New York City, but I learned my lessons through your replacement because you are no longer with me.

Unknown

You talk about the world of discoveries, with a chest of gold and gems, speaking truth to power with your chest to your beloved soulmate.

Bathing in her insecurities, while you lie and lay in the same sheets, lies the unknown; pillows that scream, echos of her childhood, but you tend to unpack her traumas in a box stored away on layaway.

Layers of damage have been done, yet you are there to restore and pick up her baggage at your doorstep to heal her into a new person.

He loves in prayer, private, and public, as she becomes the rising Phoenix she was destined to be, but both of them hold passions through their flesh; their bones; gazing through each other's eyes, as the Milky Way intertwines no corruption with their revised version—of not knowing the steps to climb Mt. Everest to reach the heaven gates.

But somehow they both took a leap of faith, with their eyes closed.

Whirlpool

Swirling water when two opposing currents meet is a collision of sweet love. Captured in a vortex of his serene physical touch. I wonder how convulsive tides fall and rise, although we fall and rise together, as a higher power builds us up, and we somehow break each other down…

His tongue is the paintbrush to my chocolate milk body, while he slowly licks me up and down, as if I'm french toast sticks with cinnamon, and he puts his syrup on top.

Tangoing the night away as we push and pull each other's emotions to another coplanar strip-line. We aren't doing this on purpose, but there is a purpose during the Autumn season, while water is going through the Glen Canyon Dam to cool our anger down.

Even if I can't stand you at the moment, let my tongue explain how much I missed you. Caught up in the maelstrom of sensations during a misty, matutinal, smoky Sunday drinking the taste of your Lychee Purple Tea made from the Lavender nectar of your lips.

Trying to find my way back to you is a task, mainly because you're everywhere, but nowhere. You're trying to find your way back to me, but my feelings flew away on a JetBlue Airplane to the beautiful Congo. Seeing each other is like koi fish dancing in a tsunami—we would never reach each other physically, but we will reach each other spiritually.

Animosity

Strong desires of hostility as I scribble some calligraphy into some methamphetamine into his liver, now we are both damaged. Hurt from the false promises you made, telling me to take another shot, as you take a toast to poverty, and I take a shot to his back to black spinning until I beat the shot clock.

Conspiring to graph his location and plot his coordinates, so no more footprints can catch my drift. Aston Martin Vantage GT4 dragging as I draft across his heart removing the bandage he once placed there for protection.

Thinking about you lost in a world with no love, peace, and direction, while figuring out how to examine the Eros and Athena in his eyes. Got hit in the crossfire with himself because he hates how I can move on with or without him.

Murder She Wrote

Murder she wrote across her lips whenever she kissed her hardworking husband goodnight, as the full moon rises. Hallow, yet magical, the sky was slowly becoming Sacramento Green and earthy. So innocent, however; she's evil and conniving wearing her red bottom stilettos and kinky curly afro, glazing her fingers transversely on his chest.

She knows that she's a distraction. Forbidden from the Garden of Eden, but tempts her husband every time with her candy-red apple lips and curvaceous figure.

Poisoned him with the words that she spews to him in his right ear and poisoned by the taste of her seductive personality, while she twirls her coils. He wants to feel like he's arrested for her love, but she's arresting her heart out of her hatred for him.

She got him back written in blood. Spinning the block several times with her toxic ways to break him to pieces. He does not know what peace is.

Although she disturbs him, he still thinks his wife is perfect beyond measure. She only wants to get it back in blood. Wearing a ski mask to hide her true intentions, she kills her husband's soul and ego. She had the nerve to paint his name in the Sacramento Green sky.

Overwhelmed

I feel the weight of the deranged world on my
shoulders.
It's starting to get heavy.
Six to ten pearl river boulders use its juniper
monster claws like a pungent blade to tempt me
to see a glacier and to be it—cold and still.
The cherry blood on my back and the crimson
blood on my shirt are the I-95 Expressway to
depression, anxiety, and insomnia.

Playing checkers instead of chess with my chest,
be sure to have a lock and throw away the key.
Recreate a composition piece on a piano to hear
minor 7th chords toying with my
discography—"Mind-Blowing",
"SUBMERGED", and "Overpower" with
contrasting sentiments.

Drowning beneath,
defeated completely,
A typhoon I cried in Atlantis as I wiped my
stresses away.

The Truth About Monsters

Dear Green Monster,
Am I horrible for having skeletons in my closet?
I mean doesn't everybody have them?
Look to my left to do the right things, but a wave of guilt and jealousy comes over me. Uncontrollable at times, my tongue tends to lash out my projections onto others. There are demons to fight, but they are afraid of me too.
How do I deal with you?
Sincerely,
An adult trying to figure out the world

Dear young adult,
I'm the monster in your head if you haven't learned yet. I cause self-destruction at the push of a button. Yes, I cause your self-esteem to sink to the bottom of the ocean where the sun doesn't shine. But since I'm not today, I won't tell you how to get rid of me, only how to tolerate me. You have to stop comparing yourself to others all of the time. The skeletons I left in the closet were burnt friendships, relationships, and partnerships you burnt due to your rage of jealousy keeping in your mind. Yes everyone has them, but it's how you deal with them moving

forward. Being envious is not the way to go.
Even the Grinch has a certain level of empathy.
That is, what you will do with that information.
Sincerely,
The Green Monster

Indigo

Witnessed the flame from a Pacific Grove candle, a color so dark—purplish blue pulsing through my arteries. You don't cry as you used to through the hopefulness of depression. Remission into the sorrows of the candle's light dimming my happy thoughts into ash. Travel to the Indigo River where starry nights exist and aren't a figment of the imagination. Alone to exist with or without my deepest self, blues and rhythms overthink just like my anxiety.

Red

Sirens for signs of help blaring.
Try again to focus on the task at hand.
Embarrassed to argue back.
Dance with Satan since you love thee.
Angry that you neglected and left me in the cold.

Autumn Feelings

Not awake tonight.
Peaceful pastimes we feel;
chill breeze floats away.

Spring

Weeds spin on their new 18-inch wheels to death, the piquant smell of the Ghost Orchid who glided away—the Blue Puya that spread their petals like an Indian Peafowl—and the kaleidoscopic patterns in a Middlemist Red Camellia echos into the meadows.

The richness of soil races into the Majorelle Garden, bringing fortune to those who water it. Sprung out of bed to watch the view of breathtaking scenery, peaceful to the mind, and pleasant for the ears. It is worthy of love and life.

Burning Bridges

We cut ties,
as the knife runs deep through the Waxing Gibbons
Moon and our pockets,
turning from lovable friends to fighting foes.
Paying the price for your betrayal at the cost of my
dignity and self-worth,
while your conscious fed me to the wolves.

My loyalty lies within my heart but flows within your
soul.
Planted the seeds in the ground for our friendship to
grow,
just for pesticides to keep our friendship stagnant.

Crying out for help,
but wasn't screaming loud enough.
I didn't want to hurt you in the process,
while I was protecting you.
Flaming carmine red infernos and violent flames are
the evil pathways to my enemies.

You all have demons,
while I make friends with my grim reapers.
Broken promises are the shadow of you.
Human nature breaks the tangible and intangible by
burning bridges.

The Irony of It All

I used to take the blame for you no matter what. No matter if I was up or I was feeling stuck. Handed you a shamrock for good luck and fortune. The opposite happened to me, now I keep having misfortunes.

Picked up your crosses, while you were getting crossed by your family. Sometimes I wondered what would happen if I would have packed my luggage with my emotions and thrown it off the balcony. Searching for my mind, deep in the gutter, suffered from insanity.

At a crossroads between me, myself, and I, when I hopped on the train and the next stop was my "Vanity of Human Wishes". Fishing in the Atlantic Ocean for the old you.

I wore a mask to heal the scars you never gave me a preview. Lights, cameras, action—consistently was a great actor, and liar. Had all my feelings on fire with no ice though.

All the things I've seen, you always wanted to perform on Broadway. The only difference was the end scene ended up in the hallway. Wrong place and the wrong time.

I don't smoke weed, I smoke people. Swish them around, I know that's evil. You tased my heart like a taser and now I can never forgive you for what you've done to me.

Now that we are no longer friends, we step into our truths and different points of view.

Birthday Cake

Blow your candles out and make a wish to reverse time because you do not want to look or feel older, but birthday cakes are no anti-aging cream. Buttercream frosting and blueberry ice cream on the side, fill her gluttony and lust, while she cheats on her husband with Sweetermen of different tiers for their bread.

A high volume of confetti sprinkles pours onto the cake each time she lies to her husband, with her sugar bliss lips, for he is blinded by love. Congratulations, it's a boy, to find out the child is not his and now he's carrying his baggage to the airport to get checked, while he has gone to therapy to get in check.

That baby boy is going to have to blow his candles out and make a wish to reverse his mother's wrongdoings and wishes to know his abandoned father. Birthday cake is not an anti-again cream, so the boy who's now a grown man, celebrates his birthdays with sweet revenge, cream cheese frosting, and coconut ice cream on the side, to fill his vengefulness, lustful, and disrespectful thoughts of women to get back at his mom for causing his pain.

Cotton Candy Ice Cream

Cotton Candy Ice Cream is for life's winners who climb Mt. Everest with their bare calloused hands, as they passionately allow their hearts to become their compass and guide their minds to become a roadmap to achieve their goals.

While I daydream outside my window during a scorching summer day, as it sold pink Himalayan salt and shared its sputtering circuit of energy, I charged up when the Mister Softee ice cream truck fluttered to the end of my block. Reminders of the circle of life start to flash before my eyes, as I see myself transitioning into adulthood. Say goodbye to the innocence we had during our childhood and hello to this cold world we know of.

Grabbed a cone of new adventures hoping it doesn't melt on my grey t-shirt with anxiety and unhappiness. I start to become overwhelmed with loneliness, so I eat rum and raisins to raise my spirits. It's more precious than liquid gold. It's life's precious moments we cherish like our first love, even though I feel guilty for using your C.R.E.A.M. Addicted to your rockin' and popping nature, I can't just quit cold Turkey Hill to save me.

Especially because of the Ben and Jerry's partnership we had due to pain and pleasure, but newfound luck could be found in Breyer's ice cream.

Time Meets Adulthood

May I love a sharp adulthood of absurd time?
Aim– clock composed miserable numbers
paralyzed now, as oak emerging from nature.

Xanthite

Xeroradiographs show the X-ray skeletons of
xenial destinations on a quest using a
xebec to float your desires away.
Xylophones whistle to the songs of your beauty,
while
xenocurrency is the epitome of your richness,
but
xeriscaping your personality for others to digest
is not you.

www.ingramcontent.com/pod-product-compliance
Lightning Source LLC
Chambersburg PA
CBHW051749130826
49812CB00033B/1068
* 9 7 8 9 3 5 7 4 4 0 7 9 0 *